# THIS CHANGES EVERYTHING

Christina Starobin

# DEDICATION

This book is dedicated to the wonderful medical staff who kept me alive and who keep countless others alive and to my family and friends who supported me through this and continue to gladden my life.

# ACKNOWLEDGEMENTS

"no such thing as a good shot" appeared in <u>War Crimes Times</u>, Nov. 2010.

# Contents

# THIS CHANGES EVERYTHING

# This changes everything

Positively
Having the virus & bronchitis

I am hopeful
But doubtful

Don't call, I can't talk
Sore throat, sentimental
If I don't e-mail or text

You'll understand

I'll meet you on the other side
Of this illness
Or perhaps I'll visit
Your thoughts

Thank you thank you thank you

—11/27/20

# Inside the Covid hospital

Inside the Covid hospital
There is disease
There is silence

No one wants to hear the news
Those who mock the
Disease they are fighting

Blue plastic gowns & gloves
Go on & off
Every time you need anything, a soda, water
Someone must put on
Protective clothing

There is TV
There are meals
There are greetings, "feel better"

There is the regimen of
Shift change & medication
 & blood work

Inside the hospital
There is silence

—12/18/20

# The vaccine

Across the land
Little vials
Speed their way into
The blood stream of

The essential workers
Little miracle workers
On the TV

People getting their shots

Again, again!
My nurse is a TV star
Hallelujah!

America will be healthy again!
Can't get enough!
Another shot! Another shot!

Another!
The bodies cry out,
Protect me! Protect me!

—12/19/20

# My love

Since I cannot embrace you
Take the dawning day
As my open arms

The birds bring my kisses

If the day is overcast
It is because you are not
By my side

But the winds in the trees
Carry all my heart's love
To caress you

As the night comes
Count one more day
Closer to when
We can again embrace

My love, my happiness

& I will again feel whole

—12/21/21

# It's hard to behave when you think your life's at stake

Afterwards you want to apologize
Yourself revealed in chances you're forced to take

The plasma ordered could be your lucky break
In demand, what if it can't arrive?
It's hard to behave when you think your life's at stake

Put it out of mind—hope can be a snake
Like the oxygen tubing; accidentally it ties
Yourself revealed in chances you're forced to take

Don't try to think; that is a mistake
All your energy is need to survive
It's hard to behave when you think your life's at stake

There is no choice of what you might forsake
Time dissolves while waiting to revive
Yourself revealed in chances you're forced to take

And finally you almost have to fake
The optimism that you will remain alive
It's hard to behave when you think your life's at stake
Yourself revealed in chances you're forced to take

—1/29/21

# To those who are not yet born

We could not describe
Living through this time

The fear, the outrage, the unexpected
Reversals

As if you were a teacup
& the table cloth pulled
Out from under you

Or the cable on the
Elevator
Cut
Free fall

Where will it stop—

Or finding kindness
When most needed

Or hope
That this will not
Last forever

—11/3/20

# Falling into the pit of despond

Unfamiliar blank walls
With nothing beyond

If you can breathe
If you can breathe

Jet plane up your nose
No thought of what
Comes
Next

Suddenly a man sticks his
Head in the door
"Phil & the whole class of
HR71 send their love"

"How strange!  The nurse has
The same class as I do"

Then I realized—it was
For me!

You had found me!
What great delight!
Someone came for me!

And then began the
Invisible angels supporting
Me, lifting me on
Pink clouds of joy

Above the metal bed
The machines the
Blood work the
Interminable search for

Non-existent veins

Always there to carry me
Carry me without fear
& the letters!

No one receives mail here

Addresses, the pictures of
Sunflowers, brilliant birds,
Vermeer, Monet
The addresses from all over
For me! For me!

And to be the official poet laureate!
More than I hoped or dreamed
Carrying me
Me!

A light through the window
Finding me
Somehow I will not die here

A band of angels
Coming after me
Coming for to carry me home

—12/21/21

# IN THE EVENT OF MY DEATH, SOME THOUGHTS

# The town I live in

Vanishes
My job, the book
I was reading
The corner I

Just turned
The difficulty I was
So near to
Solving

The opinions of
Those I had offended

All gone

As soon as
I awake

# The ride of a lifetime

The same infinity
The next infinity
The last infinity

It's all one,
Isn't it?

Wrap your mind
Around it like a
Mobius strip

Here we go
Up the rollercoaster and
Down—
Whee!

# Instantaneous

The tiny mice teeth
Of time
& their little black droppings

So far from the geese

Squawking flying regrouping
In huge V's
Overhead

Affirming
Eternity

# Houses at night

People light their windows
& we see inside

The magic beacons
Of their lives

Which they illuminate for us
To see our lives

Beacons of the lives
They live

& cannot see

# Gift

Together you are all of me
The sky the sea the fields the mountains
Together we breathe to be
Unexpected rushing forth the fountain

And on & on we always go
The rain the wind the catastrophe
The healing the silence the mountain snow
Until the untold tale is free

And what we'll learn & what we'll love
Ages ages have known & lost
& we will find it all again
& boundless joy will be the cost

# For W. M.

This time of year
We look forward &
Back at once

With hope, with love,
Fondness & energy to
Begin

We do not imagine
Death or if we
Expect it, it
Still surprises us

In that one instant
Our attention
Is elsewhere

Telling us, "Do not
Take me for granted;
Life cannot be
Ignored."

Walter, you outlived
So many, despite
Hardships, disease,
Constant vigilance,

Your love for others
Sustained our
Constant joy &

Sense of continuity,
That everything is all right.

You leave us with
Gratitude for having
Known you &

Begin again
Never taking love & life
For granted.

# There's a secret way to dig a grave

You must make an agreement
with the earth.
 "Let me move you. You
are important & must make way."

Tell the stones, "You have
been here long enough!"

The biggest stone has a special
importance. "You will be the
headstone—a place of
great honor!"
Then see how quickly it gives up its place!

The dirt falls away quickly now.

Death is going into another room.
The door is not always easy to open.

It takes a lifetime.

# When this road comes to an end

When this road comes to an end
All that we would wish to know
Is that our family & our friends
Are there with us when we go

From all that we have been & done
Joys, sorrows, care & strife
All that's left are memories
To carry on from this short life

& so we weep & then reflect
On the importance of love through pain
We bid farewell & then we pause
As the love in our hearts reigns

# This is your lucky day!

It starts unpropitiously—
you're late, traffic backs up

all the familiar good things
to do are left
undone

you rush into
the unknown

& it's great!

A stranger lavishes
You with unexpected praise

All the 17 buffalo
Are grazing so close
To your car you can't
Even see them
So  you double back
& watch
The wind ruffling their hair
 Their curved horns
You hit the jackpot!

Your favorite song
Is on the radio
What you thought

A mistake
Was the right thing after all

You flush
Three owls
From their perches

& you don't know
What  happens
Next

# When you read

Time evaporates.  You
Don't go places
But when you
Stop the time

Is gone.

Space journey
Instantaneous

Now
Where had the
Time gone?

# The arriving rainbow

A surprise
In front of your eyes

At first & last sight
To the left & then the right

Beginning to fade
It comes again bright
It's made & unmade
& everything's right

For a moment we breathe
As the rainbow bequeaths
Divinity to all
It holds in its thrall

# The embroidery of newly fallen snow

Layers of branches with white icing

No one has walked here
But the deer

No wind has disturbed
The infinite tracery

But suddenly a blob
Falls

# How many movies

How many movies
Do you have in your head?

The way it felt so close
That bedroom window
Of your childhood

The cool satin edges
Of your blanket

Sitting at the desk
In grade school

The first time you met
Your dog

The waiting line at the airport
Shoveling snow
Cardinals flying across your path

These movies are far more
Important than the ones
Made by others

They go into you
Like a nail hammered
Into your
Soul

You inhale them like hunger

# When you come to the end

When you come to the end
Of arguing
Of preparing & using &
Cleaning up
Of achieving & recognizing
& helping others realize

When you come to the end
Of appreciating
Of losing & finding
Of aggravation
Of tears & outrage
Of illness & recovery
Of forgetting & remembering

Where everyone you know is
Dead & they are
Waiting to welcome you

Then you take your
Lover's hand & go
Forward with delight

# One day

One day, as if by
Accident, I will
Find that button in the book-
Case opening

The secret room
Where all the bad
Decisions will be proved

To be right
All the noise will
Become music & all

The evil ones will be
Vaporized & the

Name on the button is
"no more war"
& the name of the
Room is
NOW

# Who will close the book

Who will close the book on
my life?
What will be the final
Chapter?

Will I be the
Heroine? A comedienne?
Comic-tragic?

What will be the
Consensus?
Can I see the reviews?

Will there be a movie?
A sequel?

Will you
Be there?

# VILLANELLES PLUS

# You are the constellations of my heart

You are the constellations of my heart
I know that you will always grace my sky
To guide me when we're near or far apart

I can't mark the date exactly of the start
I know your death settled you on high
You are the constellations of my heart

And then when others were added to the chart
Not dead but moved so still they were nearby
To guide me when we're near or far apart

So you change positions as seasons depart
Or if it's cloudy or in the day you'll fly
You are the constellations of my heart

Look up in the sky; there is an art
& science knowing names you are known by
To guide me when we're near or far apart

My names are personal & when a hurt smarts
Or I need to share a joy or be counseled why
You are the constellations of my heart
To guide me when we're near or far apart
—2015

# Anglo-Saxon riddle poem:  what am I?

Stretching heartbeats, end to end, I hear
Something I've been struggling to forget
The ocean sound & hoof beats running clear

So clotted with errands far & near
Our purpose dimmed, buried deep & yet
Stretching heartbeats, end to end, I hear

In perfect silence illusions disappear
As does desire, repentance & regret
The ocean sound & hoof beats running clear

Or in the snow, the hoof prints of the deer
Show me the path of what's escaped the net
Stretching heartbeats, end to end, I hear

How could I replace the chandelier
Of night sky with its crystal secret?
The ocean sound & hoof beats running clear

All come together, wildness now appears
& takes off!  The decades' super jet
Stretching heart beats, end to end, I hear
The ocean sound & hoof beats running clear

Answer:  I am an electrocardiogram.

# In the prison of each declining hour

In the prison of each declining hour
Where strengths & downfalls unexpected show
All delight & sorrow come to flower

Witnessed from the highest winding tower
The boats & tiny people in them row
In the prison of each declining hour

Replay your memories, do not cower
The pattern appears as lights in twilight glow
All delight & sorrow come to flower

What we thought sweet curdles & is sour
We revolt from pleasures thrice bestowed
In the prison of each declining hour

What will emerge to adorn the heart's bower ?
Shameless sunrise?  The riot of the snow?
All delight & sorrow come to flower

Who am I & wherefore comes this power?
Who are you whom I have come to know?
In the prison of each declining hour
All delight & sorrow come to flower

# Never  thinking as we move along

Never thinking as we move along
Through taken for granted tasks & special times
These thoughts remain when time itself is gone

Unexpectedly, a radio song
Ignites, like 50 years ago, our spirit's climb
Never thinking as we move along

How going to the market, right or wrong,
Would resonate so deeply, a golden chime
These thoughts remain when time itself is gone

We watch & plan to make ourselves belong
In our lives, we prepare the rhyme
Never thinking as we move along

The outcome we foresee, weak or strong,
Is  not something either yours or mine
These thoughts remain when time itself is gone

We cannot hold but catch amid the throng
Minutes cascading in relentless brine
Never thinking as we move along
These thoughts remain when time itself is gone

# On my birthday

Do years fly south like geese & then return
All youthful days restore, not fade away
And reunited, lovers, no more to yearn?

Why cannot the time remain the greenest fern
Though hidden from our sight like night the day?
Do years fly south like geese & then return?

Like waterfalls replenished the parched berms
Now rains to nourish fields of waiting hay
And reunited, farmers no more to yearn

Or bellies fat in summer, fat will burn
To keep us winter warm as skins turn grey
Do years fly south like geese & then return?

Can you not forget what you have learned
And let a fresher vision return to stay
And reunited, lovers no more to yearn?

So cycles spin our lives, turn & turn
Joy & sorrow, empty/full, now toil now play
Do years fly south like geese & then return
And reunited, lovers no more to yearn?

# No matter how, when you're sick you lose

no matter how, when you're sick you lose
medicine's a bore & then there's stress
waiting in the doctor's office blues

if you don't know what you've got don't confuse
the doctor with symptoms upon which to muse
take off your coat & shirt, your pants & shoes

he'll order tests & then he will peruse
the results; always answer "yes"
waiting in the doctor's office blues

if treatment is slow, don't bruise
his ego; don't argue his diagnosis
take off your coat & shirt, your pants & shoes

do what you're told; you cannot choose
forget your ideas of health you once possessed
waiting in the doctor's office blues

someday maybe you'll hear the happy news
your health has been restored, more or less
waiting in the doctor's office blues
take off your coat & shirt, your pants & shoes

## 111.  where does knowledge come from? where does it go?

where does knowledge come from? where does it go?
is it a light? a book? a story? a jewel?
if you could know one thing, what would you know?

is it something someone can bestow?
like a teacher when you go to school?
where does knowledge come from?  where does it go?

or is it gained by wandering to & fro?
testing the exception to the rule?
if you could know one thing, what would you know?

or will it appear by magic like the snow
and transform us, or unravel like a spool?
where does knowledge come from?  where does it go?

or like the sunrise with widening glow
will we awake to find ourselves the fool?
if you could know one thing, what would you know?

unexpected, sudden this rainbow
will heal all horrors & our doubts so cruel
where does knowledge come from?  where does it go?
if you could know one thing, what would you know?

—2/23/11

# 112. unsuspecting as we glance into the sky

unsuspecting we glance into the sky
in the ordinary path of day
there, wide winged, white head, the eagle flies

for just a moment, who knows why,
we avert our eyes another way
unsuspecting we glance into the sky

how magnificent what we espy!
our momentary chance is thus repaid
there, wide winged, white head, the eagle flies

how could we forget or even try
once seeing this over-splendid display?
unsuspecting we glance into the sky

wings a steady line, open wide
tail whiter than the mountain snow arrayed
there, wide winged, white head, the eagle flies

who do we become when we die
in our minds, more wondrous?  who can say?
unsuspecting we glance into the sky
there, wide winged, white head, the eagle flies

—2/23/11

## 113.  a simple pattern:  up & down, up & down

a simple pattern:  up & down, up & down
do not allow your mind to be misled
all of life:  round & round & round

little infants, we have always found,
sleep & cry until they are well fed
a simple pattern:  up & down, up & down

the seasons pass triumphant with no sound
the buds, the flowers, leaves, the snowy beds
all of life:  round & round & round

& when you're ill, or thinking, nerves are wound
so tight you cannot stay in bed
a simple pattern:  up & down, up & down

approach the end of life above the ground
joy & sadness alternate instead
all of life:  round & round & round

for those who remain the memories abound
we know too well what lies ahead
a simple pattern:  up & down, up & down
all of life:  round & round & round

—2/26/11

## 114.  the ice show is over; let's begin

the ice show is over; let's begin
the swim games, the flower show & more
we're either losers, or we all will win

two inches of rain gave us all a spin
& melting icebergs left us ponds galore
the ice show is over; let's begin

first clear the decks, make it trim
mopping up the water on the floor
we're either losers, or we all will win

strategies may differ; the river's rim
floats all away, hear the waves roar!
the ice show is over; let's begin

no matter how we're grieving or grim
let's celebrate the welcome change in store
we're either losers, or we all will win

my mind's a carnival, hear the din!
like aerialists, trapeze to trapeze we'll soar!
the ice show is over; let's begin
we're either losers, or we all will win

   —3/7/11,

# 115.  comforted by spirits I have known

comforted by spirits I have known
even those who led me so astray
I settle in my earth-lit, star-bound home

the mermaid with her golden comb
was grandmother's gift as in  bed she lay
& read to me of sea tides' magic foam

nor was she destined to remain alone
other stories joined in swift relay
peopling my childhood from the well-worn tomes

my father took me through the time zones
of space plus time & taught me to delay
thinking things through in a way quite his own

grandfather gave me strength, although on loan
til I could find my own stance to repay
the gifts the winds of worlds have surely blown

so many others through my life have roamed
& helped me to chart/rechart my way
comforted by spirits I have known
I settle in my earth-lit, star-bound home

—3/8/11

# 116. my dog is dying; there's nothing I can do

my dog is dying; there's nothing I can do
make him cozy, show him all my love
what if it were me?  what if it were you?

I remember our walks, mornings, evenings, too
he'd turn his head & stare at me above
my dog is dying; there's nothing I can do

if love has no end or start in view
except when it hits you like a club
what if it were me?  what if it were you?

all the moments pass in quick review
you took my life & gave me quite a shove
my dog is dying; there's nothing I can do

how large a dog, I ask you true,
will replace you in my heart, that's the rub!
what if it were me?  what if it were you?

without you I'll be incomplete, a shoe
without its mate, a lonely glove
my dog is dying; there's nothing I can do

if you get better a bird that flew
into my life & I can't get enough
my dog is dying; there's nothing I can do
what if it were me?  what if it were you?

—3/10/11

## 117. we never know what's around the bend in the river

we never know what's around the bend in the river
we start winning; we thought we'd always win
when it was good, we thought it was forever

the other side of the world begins to quiver
the earthquake you don't expect begins
we never know what's around the bend in the river

and then the tsunami, the biggest ever,
or so it seems as the water rushes in
when it was good, we thought it was forever

how can you plan to be surprised?  sever
your happy endings & perception spins
we never know what's around the bend in the river

how can we help, we who are so clever?
thousands of miles away, the Pacific rim
when it was good, we thought it was forever

the nuclear accident was the final lever
pulled to make the future more than grim
we never know what's around the bend in the river
when it was good, we thought it was forever

—3/21/11

# 118.  all the trinkets will not fill your place

all the trinkets will not fill your place
if I go through it now will it hurt as much?
I never knew there was so much empty space

all the puzzles will not resolve your fate
I figure, refigure time & space & love
all the trinkets will not fill your place

our morning walks, how can I retrace
the steps over every rock & bluff?
I never knew there was so much empty space

watching you suffer, hoping as I wait
I purchase the imagined future in the rough
all the trinkets will not fill your place

every farewell's the possible last race
be here when I return, a kiss, a touch
I never knew there was so much empty space

come stars, come planets, celestial estates
your brilliant toys will not be enough
all the trinkets will not fill your place
I never knew there was so much empty space

—4/3/11

# 120.  Then between us this shall never end

then between us this shall never end
until the last unexpected breath
I sit here on the grass with you, my friend

this morning when the hummingbird did send
its lightness to banish all regrets
then between us this shall never end

and the herons, two so simply blend
their wings & legs into the trees instead
I sit here on the grass with you, my friend

the adolescent eagle did amend
time's vista to converge the future, yet
then between us this shall never end

I will not dally nor will I pretend
now there is no planning to upset
I sit here on the grass with you, my friend

until all endings which can portend
I wait with you into the coming death
then between us this shall never end
I sit here on the grass with you, my friend

—5.8.11

## 121.  the violet rhododendron with its plumes

the violet rhododendron with its plumes
began the day you died & carries on
every day another blossom blooms

just like your eternal gifts which loom
around the corner as we chance upon
the violet rhododendron with its plumes

as you entered that dark final room
you could no longer help us to respond
every day another blossom blooms

recall the waterfall, our tiny flume
your tail, a metronome, a magic wand
the violet rhododendron with its plumes

into every room you would carom
upsetting all expectations & beyond
every day another blossom blooms

into every crevice your love zooms
& expands forward, electric rippling pond
the violet rhododendron with its plumes
every day another blossom blooms

—5/24/11

## 122.  every time I open the door I think of you

every time I open the door I think of you
where are you?  I'll see you once again
every time I return home, what can I do?

twelve years each day, together we're linked, we two
each morning walk, snow, sun, dawn & rain
every time I open the door I think of you

and how I now miss the happy view
of your tail wagging & your barked refrain
every time I return home, what can I do?

you taught me to adventure, I had no clue
how to roam, explore, enjoy the new terrain
every time I open the door I think of you

I think I see your essence through & through
in my dreams to spare me future pain
every time I return home, what can I do?

my heart's far larger now & just as blue
but win or lose I never will complain
every time I open the door I think of you
every time I return home, what can I do?

—5/31/11

# 123.  perched on a high wire, a hummingbird

perched on a high wire, a hummingbird
something's in the air flying free
red rambling roses in our yard

joy & sorrow come so fast they're blurred
walking pathways where we used to be
perched on a high wire, a hummingbird

small houses, motels, near & far
so much the same in my memory
red rambling roses in our yard

can't  you hear the message?  have you heard?
love begets love, perpetual jubilee
perched on a high wire, a hummingbird

and truth is sacred still & still & hard
forgotten graveyards that we cannot see
red rambling roses in our yard

my power place is sacred & absurd
my home is here, I take it within me
perched on a high wire, a hummingbird
red rambling roses in our yard

—6/7/11

# 124.  every magnificent voyage into the unknown

every magnificent voyage into the unknown
every one, through ages, through the miles
another form of dying, of going home

not knowing where you'll end up you roam
the different lands proffer their varied wiles
every magnificent voyage into the unknown

now there's the sea, you never are alone
whales, puffins, sea birds all the while
another form of dying, of going  home

or the sky whose art none can clone
the shifting shapes like centuries fly
every magnificent voyage into the unknown

or the caves with drawings on the stone
the buffalo, the horse, leopards all in style
another form of dying, of going home

yet all draw together in their magic form
to transport you while in awe you cry
every magnificent voyage into the unknown
another form of dying, of going home

—6/11/11

## 126.  how do you undo all the pain?

how do you undo all the pain?
useless, since your death, unraveling all
trying to stop the love or the rain

in your final illness none did explain
how each image has its sharp recall
how do you undo all the pain?

the paths we walked I can't refrain
from walking again, alone & feeling small
trying to stop the love or the rain

and the flooding basement over & over again
I bail & sop, but still the rain does fall
how do you undo all the pain?

it rained in these last months, a watery chain
linking grief & sorrow into an iron ball
trying to stop the love or the rain

that flowers come I remember again & again
to transmute to beauty, an infinitesimal crawl
how do you undo all the pain?
trying to stop the love or the rain

—7/4/11

## 128.  the manta ray undulates its way

the manta ray undulates its way
the sharks like lawyers lurk about the rocks
underwater seaweeds blend & sway

the starfish, routinely losing an arm, may
regrow itself leaving us in shock
the manta ray undulates its way

the giant squid's more deadly than they say
so please keep moving, careful what you knock
underwater seaweeds blend & sway

above the sea birds always make it pay
to venture from the unsuspecting rocks
the manta ray undulates its way

and the humpback whale & baby are at play
their tails appear when leaving while seabirds flock
underwater seaweeds blend & sway

above or below the water, night or day
the mesmerizing universe unlocks
the manta ray undulates its way
underwater seaweeds blend & sway

—7/19/11

# 129.  the arch of Cabo San Lucas

the arch of Cabo San Lucas behind it all
we zip by on the pleasure boat serene
pelicans flying back & forth, the ocean's call

the glass factory with its mosaic wall
makes a turtle drink tequila, what a scene!
the arch of Cabo San Lucas behind it all

the cactus garden radiating, standing tall
& small the spring flowers, sculpted green
pelicans flying back & forth, the ocean's call

the heat!  the heat!  makes the hours crawl
inside the church, cool shadows reign supreme
the arch of Cabo San Lucas behind it all

the artists' market beckons with its stalls
plates, beads, costumes for king or queen
pelicans flying back & forth, the ocean's call

a day of fiesta & touring as sunset falls
nostalgic for the memories we've seen
the arch of Cabo San Lucas behind it all
pelicans flying back & forth, the ocean's call

—7/10/11

# 130.  parasails like jelly fish ascend

parasails like jellyfish ascend
this harbor gives us visions of journeys new
the ocean is horizon without end

snorkeling near the rocks can upend
you when the waves play loose with you
parasails like jellyfish ascend

the hurricane made the fish suspend
their normal swimming; we only see blue
the ocean is horizon without end

when the fire dancers did pretend
there was no danger, rain soaked us through
parasails like jellyfish ascend

the boat ride back with lightning as our friend
dispossessed our notions of what was true
the ocean is horizon without end

starfish in the aquarium move like glue
we keep each separate moment; then they blend
parasails like jelly ish ascend
the ocean is horizon without end

—7/22/11

# 131. before you came I did not know that place

before you came I did not know that place
the place that dogs find in our lives & ways
now you're gone; none can fill that space

I did not know the morning's excited race
to greet the trees & fields, which joy repays
before you came I did not know that place

when you escaped & ran your unknown race
I searched & ran then cried as home I stayed
now you're gone; none can fill that space

by my side or waiting to see my face
to jump & greet me, wag the tail always
before you came I did not know that place

to sleep with me ready to erase
all disappointments which life replays
now you're gone; none can fill that space

the paths of time cannot be effaced
I rediscover as in wait love lies
before you came I did not know that place
now you're gone; none can fill that space

—8/7/11

# 132. when does it end?  who turns it off at last?

when does it end?  who turns it off at last?
a screen that shows the memories of my life
does it go slow?  now it's going fast

the starry night, the oceans ever vast
political scrabble, solidarity & strikes
when does it end?  who turns it off at last?

spilled medicine as the die is cast
regrets, hallucinations & the like
does it go slow?   now it's going fast

"carpe diem" was the medieval hype
to tell us "live before it's passed!"
when does it end?  who turns it off at last?

imagine it's your funeral from strife
what didn't you achieve?  experience?   at last?
does it go slow?  now it's going fast

or will you gracefully find respite
a mountain top surveying present futures past?
when does it end?  who turns it off at last?
does it go slow?  now it's going fast

—8/14/11

# 133.  wait & see is often wait in fear

wait & see is often wait in fear
the storm's fierce path topsy-turned our life
imagination's horrors far & near

our house survived & so did yours, we hear
but no electric makes each chore a strife
wait & see is often wait in fear

the road's blocked with trees far & near
power lines & flooding, uncertainty's rife
imagination's horrors far & near

so what becomes important?   nothing's clear
those we love, our safety, husband, wife
wait & see is often wait in fear

until a patch of blue sky won so dear
lifts our gaze & slashes with its knife
imagination's  horrors far & near

we shall look back & this will disappear
a narrative to recall & add rare spice
wait & see is often wait in fear
imagination's horrors far & near

—8/29/11

# 134. sorting through the debris with psychic heft

sorting through the debris with psychic heft
the lives & deaths, the wheel again spins round
all the time juggling what is left

today we struggling draw a deeper breath
a new dog is coming from the pound
sorting through the debris with psychic heft

in wake of illness, hurricane & death
simple forgotten treasures now are found
all the time juggling what is left

bills & will, jewelry. boots bereft
of smaller feet, we're outgrowing all around
sorting through the debris with psychic heft

medicine that prolongs & shrinks so deft
you can't tell if you're decked or crowned
all the time juggling what is left

simplify! simplify! is advice we've always kept
now under heartbeats it's the only sound
sorting through the debris with psychic heft
all the time juggling what is left

—9/7/11

# 135. All nagging disappointments swept away

all nagging disappointments swept away
the restaurant owner said, "Look! Quick!"
we saw a rainbow in the parking lot today

magic is as magic does, they say
though we spent three weeks horribly sick
all nagging disappointments swept away

the suddenness, unexpected display
the arc en ciel is no majestic trick
we saw a rainbow in the parking lot today

some took photos for a later day
to prolong the mystery, make it stick
all nagging disappointments swept away

a second rainbow began but didn't stay
we watched as it faded, then got thick
we saw a rainbow in the parking lot today

these moments we hold forever & may
from rainbow to rainbow take our pick
all nagging disappointments swept away
we saw a rainbow in the parking lot today

—9/16/11

## 136.  Time plays tricks we suddenly recall

Time plays tricks we suddenly recall
where are the promises I made?
many leaves fall.  that's not all

can it be that late?  can't I forestall
this running out of life?  this short parade?
Time plays tricks we suddenly recall

I'd planned it differently, ambitions crawl
when hit by ill health, economy, they fade
many leaves fall.  that's not all

I tried to be nice, make the right call
even if I suffered, my ideals stayed
Time plays tricks we suddenly recall

put others first, responsibilities stall
your own desire, that's how it's played
many leaves fall.  that's not all

so what is left? I face a sudden wall
that disappears into an endless glade
Time plays tricks we suddenly recall
many leaves fall.  that's not all

—9/30/11

## 137.  the things you scorn are where the rewards are

the things you scorn are where the rewards are
you're more important than your life, you say
as time runs out you run both near & far

plan a better party, get a newer car
forget what you want; toss those dreams away
the things you scorn are where the rewards are

you settle for less; how much longer til time jars
you with what you can no longer say?
as time runs out you run both near & far

who is that in the mirror over the bar
in the Folies Bergere?  you?  can you stay?
the things you scorn are where the rewards are

that picture hung above your bed; you spar
with memories.  responsibilities insist "my way!"
as time runs out you run both near & far

you look down & find in your hands a star
that glows at night & guides unseen by day
the things you scorn are where the rewards are
as time runs out you run both near & far

—10/7/11

# When at last

The further you go the memories go so deep
You cannot even name each separate layer
You fall through them as you would fall asleep

So heavy then if it is something sweet
Compressed sweetness answers like a prayer
The further you go the memories go so deep

The house, the garden in a steady sweep
Unremembered flowers blossom rare
You fall through them as you would fall asleep

Half-forgotten now a sudden heap
Faces, places confront you without care
The further you go the memories go so deep

Books, thoughts, tunes of mine now leap
Upon you as if waiting there
You fall through them as you would fall asleep

Although they're ours they are not ours to keep
They visit us a minute unaware
The further you go the memories go so deep
You fall through them as you would fall asleep

—6/28/15

# No such thing as a good shot

The morning news today says Mumbai is hot
30 killed, more injured, that is clear
The shot heard round the world is every shot

The neighbor's kid's a sniper who will spot
Our cats in his crosshairs, far or near
How can I tell my own backyard from what is not?

In Vietnam we saw the bodies in their slots
As we ate our dinners we shed our tears
The shot heard round the world is every shot

The tsunami's wreckage became our own rot
Every hour the body count we'd hear
How can I tell my own backyard from what is not?

In Iraq they hid the dead that we forgot
But still the silence makes it more severe
The shot heard round the world is every shot

Now to begin again what is never forgot
Destroy each gun, each bomb or tank, each spear
The shot heard round the world is every shot
How can I tell my own backyard from what is not?

—11/27/08

# CONCURRENT EVENTS

# When do you ask for help?

When do you ask for help?
Ahead of time so
It will be there
When you need it?

When it doesn't come
"Help now!  Now!"

When it's past time
You can't wait
Not like this again

No work
Hunger
Home?  No home

When it's too
Late to help?

Was that
Last week?

We think people exaggerate
Not the real story

When you realize
What isn't here

—10/9/20

# Hats off to Americans!

Hats off to Americans!
Who braved the lines to vote
Who sent away for ballots
& mailed them

& endured the scare campaigns
Of crooked election scams

Who waited 4 days for results
Who waited 4 years for a chance
At justice

Hats off to those
Standing at the graves of the
230,000 plus Covid dead

The abuse of our trust
The abuse of our tax dollars
The abuse of our White House
As a backdrop

Having listened to the Pied Piper
Leading us into the mountain
To shut us away

We have not gone
We remain
The work continues

Beware the racist militia
The gun toting bigots
The white supremacist
Domestic terrorists

Your day is ending
Your day has been ending
For decades

Your enemy is in the White House
Waiting to lead you astray

Time to get a job
That does not involve hate
Burn the red hats

Time to move on
& rejoice

# If they can threaten to kill you

It they can threaten to kill you
For working the polls in the election

If they can threaten to kill you
For working in the hospital's ICU

If they can threaten to kill the governor
Of a state trying to keep people safe

Or kill you for doing your job
Who is safe?

People dying in the ICU who refuse
To believe they have
An infectious disease?

People who are dying from disinformation
From listening to lies
Their lives warped by
Those in government who only want

A get out of jail free card?

Who is safe?
You can die from the virus
Or lose your mind
To the fascist poison
Seig heil
Can we tell who is infected?

The motto:
Don't do your job
Don't speak out with the truth
Don't try to help the dying

Or they will surely
Track you down
You'll be sorry
You'll be sorry if you're not sorry already

Sorry that you live in the USA
Which has suddenly changed to
A Third Reich wannabe

Have the little electronic
Earwigs eaten your mind?
Your heart, your soul?

# We draw the line

We draw the line

At the end of the year
This year everyone
Seems especially anxious

"Close the door!  Lock the locks!
Trash the past!  Not
Going back there!"

340,000 plus dead
Little rodents gnawing at the
Constitution, nibbling at
Voting rights

Gloating over the pornographic
Past of lynchings & old deaths

"Keep your Dixie cups,
The South will rise again!"

But not as skeletal warriors
Sown from dragon's teeth

The South will rise
Black & proud
Tear down the concentration camps

At the border along with
The monuments

So the year end bells
Clang like the doors of
A hundred jail cells
Waiting for the old crew
To find their new lodgings

Who will survive?
Will the vaccine save us?
The new administration

The unexpected strength of
A people awakening
Makes the earth & heavens
Tremble with joy

# Bad news

Reality doesn't play by the rules
Reality doesn't listen to the
Polls, the statistics which
Percentage will vote
The way we want or don't want

Reality doesn't reason "what if?"

Reality thumbs its nose at Mother Knows Best,
Gives a finger to "Let's relax for
A minute because it's really all right"

Reality says, "Life is good" is for suckers
"It's all good" is for idiots

A new cell phone won't
Connect you to your party

There is no new app
For new apps

Money won't even
Buy you money
Love is not
There for everyone
Change your attitude if you want;
Change won't get you a new shirt for your
Funeral

The Grim Reaper is around the
Corner selling the answers
You don't want to hear
Because there are no answers

The questions stopped
Being real so long ago their

Dust has blown away

& we are standing
Watching a fast
Car escaping with all
We once thought
Was something

# The cabinet's a clown car, to be sure

The cabinet's a clown car, to be sure
Unpacking one by one the world's rejects
How much more fun can we endure?

If bad hair, prejudice & evil lies can't ensure
The judgment of the president elect
The cabinet's a clown car, to be sure

His business holdings alone, a guided tour
Of conflicting interests the world can select
How much more fun can we endure?

Every hour a new yes man adds allure
To this antidote to sanity & respect
The cabinet's a clown car, to be sure

What act can follow?  Find a cancer cure?
Or burn the Constitution they reject?
How much more fun can we endure?

Will you approve this fiasco de jour?
"Was this once my country?" you reflect
The cabinet's a clown car, to be sure
How much more fun can we endure?

—2017

# We lived in the good time

We lived in the good time
Before gene splicing
Total surveillance
Political polls
Know all you buy
Who you call
E-mail hacked

We lived in Woodstock
Sex-drugs-rock 'n roll

Before AIDS
Hep-C
Astronomy in medical costs
Cholesterol tapping
Eco-trash compacting
Can't have fun because plastics pollute the landfill

We adored the stars
Absorbed their majesty
Loved rainbows, cats & dogs & whales
Without thinking of all the ramifications

We were free

If you have found this
We are gone
You can't track us
But marvel that we existed

# To Republicans who defend Trump's insurrection

Imagine you are at home
With your family & your
Extended family, wife, husband,
Grandparents, children

Sisters, brothers & their families
Imagine you are together
To celebrate a memorable day

Say a 50$^{th}$ wedding anniversary
The golden anniversary

& as you are lifting glasses in
A toast

A battering ram breaks down your
Front door
A mob invades the living room

Yelling, chanting, brandishing pipes & poles
Pressing brothers to the walls
Choke holds on teenagers

Calling to lynch your grandparents
Breaking furniture
Standing on the tables
Mocking you

Stealing laptops
Stealing personal papers

& you say nothing?
You're giving your approval
To this?

You invite them in
Take photos with them

Show them around your
House, the people's house?
This gains your tacit approval?

I don't think so
& you don't either

—1/14/21

# Hearts explode in violence on TV

Hearts explode in violence on TV
Or are shown in slow motion
In open heart surgery

As the machines breathe slowly

We see hearts in the eyes
Of the commercial children
As they watch their dog
Or cat eat pet food

In the eyes of the girl
Getting the diamond
From her mate

We do not see the hearts
Healing because

This takes a long long time

Longer than the gravel falling
Into the grave
Longer than the bodies' decay
& the bones disappearing

Longer than your days, months
Decades
Making the memory smooth like
 A leather belt or purse
Longer than it took to grow

Civilizations explode, are destroyed
In days
Families shatter, economies are
Cracked into a million parts

Together we can help heal
Slowly like water dripping in a pond
Like a petal falling

Like an embryo growing

Like trust, respect, love growing
Suddenly the unexpected
Accumulation of a long
Process
Finally completed
Hearts healing hearts
People helping people

The world turning into the
Work turning into the
World turning

—7/29/11

# On watching the ceremony honoring the over 400,000 Covid dead

Months ago
I worked for a national day of remembrance
For the Covid dead
My efforts failed

Certain states have made remembrance

Now the reflecting pool is lit
With 400 eloquent candles
Each for 1,000 dead

& a Covid nurse
Sings "Amazing Grace" as she did
In her hospital

Flags for all those who cannot
Be present
Are lined up behind the pool

What line did I cross
That put me here
Watching
& not among the dead?

Which  candle would I be?

How many more
Candles will be lit?

—1/19/21

www.ingramcontent.com/pod-product-compliance
Lightning Source LLC
LaVergne TN
LVHW051459170726
843492LV00002B/725